Even *More* Embarrassing

DAD
JOKES

Pavilion
An imprint of HarperCollins*Publishers* Ltd
1 London Bridge Street
London SE1 9GF

www.harpercollins.co.uk

HarperCollins*Publishers*
Macken House,
39/40 Mayor Street Upper,
Dublin 1
D01 C9W8

10 9 8 7 6 5 4 3 2

First published in Great Britain by Pavilion, an imprint of
HarperCollins*Publishers* Ltd 2023

Copyright © 2023

This book is an amalgamation of material from *Bad Dad Jokes* and *Very Embarrassing
Dad Jokes Part 2* (Ian Allen) with all the good ones thrown out.
Terrible additional material by Andrew Davies.

ISBN 978-0-008604-08-0

This book is produced from independently certified FSC™ paper to ensure
responsible forest management.

For more information visit:
www.harpercollins.co.uk/green

Printed and bound in the UK using 100% renewable electricity at CPI Group (UK) Ltd

Even *More* Embarrassing

DAD JOKES

SO BAD THEY'RE ACTUALLY GOOD

Ian Allen

PAVILION

Hello again!

When I compiled the first book of Dad Jokes it was pointed out by many readers that some of the jokes were far too funny, in fact some of them almost made them break into a smile. Obviously this was a serious error.

I can only apologize to anyone who found any of the jokes in *Very Embarrassing Dad Jokes* amusing, and assure you that no stone has been left unturned to rectify the situation. In fact, I have gone to great lengths to uncover the most awful jokes possible for this follow-up. If you do by some accident find yourself laughing at anything within these pages, please contact your general practitioner, as there must be something wrong with you.

Why, you may ask, does the world need another joke book, especially one full of terrible gags like these? Well, as someone once said, 'Even the longest jokes are better than the shortest wars.' And to prove it there are some longer jokes featured in these pages – and while I've had to tell them as briefly as possible, any dad worth his salt should be able to spin out the signalman joke, for example, to a tale that would give the Anglo-Zanzibar War of 1896, which lasted just under 40 minutes, a run for its money.

And why are these dad jokes so terrible? It's because dads can't tell jokes – but they think they can. Scientists have proven the average dad is 57% less funny than he thinks he is, making it perfectly pointless to waste good material on them. So the world needs more bad dad jokes to keep them away from the good ones. You see, there's only one thing worse than your Dad telling loads of useless jokes, and that's him telling the same few over and over and over again. For instance, when my daughter was little the only joke she could remember to repeat to us was:

Why did the banana go to the doctor?
Because he wasn't peeling very well.

She told this joke so many times that it led to the formation of a brand-new family joke:

What did the doctor say to the banana?
Not you again!

And I also feel qualified to inform you that the classic dad joke should have the potential to baffle your kids for years. Consider this one:

Q. What's the difference between a duck?
A. One of its legs is both the same.

Now, when they are very young, your kids may laugh just at the nonsense of this joke. When they are a bit older they may laugh because, though they still don't get it, they think they ought to and don't want to let on. When they are older still, they may laugh just out of sympathy for the decrepit old creature that told it. But by this time, hopefully, Pavlov's Law will have taken effect and you will only have to utter the words, 'What's the difference between a duck?' for them to roll around on the floor in hysterics.

They will hate you for it, naturally, but they won't be able to stop themselves and, in due course, they will repeat the procedure with their own children. And so the cycle will turn ...

This book is proof, if proof were needed, that Dads just aren't as funny as they think they are. So, kids, grit your teeth and brace yourself for another onslaught. And Dads, get ready for another battle in your constant war on humour, and embarrass your kids with pride.

Let the jokes commence!

Teacher: That was a very interesting talk by the local undertaker. Does anyone have any questions?

Pupil: Why do they nail down the lids on coffins?

People say you should spend every day as though it's your last day on earth.

So far I've said goodbye to the cat 643 times.

Crime in multi-story car parks.

It's wrong on so many levels.

Why are farmers the biggest magicians out there?

They can turn a cow into a field.

Lucy: Every time I take my dog to the park, the ducks try to bite him.

Lauren: That's terrible. Are the ducks aggressive?

Lucy: No, I bought a dog that was pure bread.

Knock, Knock.

Who's there?

Alex

Alex who?

Alex plain later, just open the door!

Grandpa: I've got a brilliant new hearing aid, very high-tech. It's perfect, I can hear everything crystal clear.

Dad: Is it digital?

Grandpa: Half-past four.

What's the difference between a gooseberry farmer and a pirate?

A gooseberry farmer treasures his berries...

Why did the man with a bad back go to Egypt?
To see his Cairo-practor.

What's hairy and sneezes?
A coconut with a cold.

First man: The idiot trying to cross the lake on a settee is now halfway across.

Second man: Yes, sofa so good

A concerned pensioner rang her 90-year-old husband while he was driving:
'Albert, be careful, they've just said on the radio there's someone driving the wrong way on the M6.'
'I'm on the M6 now,' he replied. 'But there's not just one going the wrong way – there's hundreds of them!'

If tin whistles are made out of tin, what are fog horns made of?

Man: Could you tell me where the self-help section is, please?

Librarian: I could, but that would defeat the object.

How do you mend a broken crab?

With crab paste.

Man: Can I have an asteroid pasty, please.

Butcher: What do you mean, an asteroid pasty?

Man: Well, like the one you sold me yesterday, only a little meteor.

Teacher: Ollie, you've spent the whole lesson drawing a pair of stoats.

Ollie: Sorry miss, I'm two-weaselly distracted.

What happened to the stupid Eskimo who lit a fire in his canoe to keep warm?

He discovered that you can't have your kayak and heat it.

Here are the latest football scores:

Real Madrid 2, Surreal Madrid *fish*

What do you call a vampire with asthma?

Vlad the inhaler.

What's green and not very heavy?

Light green.

Why did the sword-swallower swallow an umbrella?

He wanted to put something away for a rainy day.

What lives under a bridge, eats goats and sings?

The big bad troll-ol-ol.

What do you call a vampire leading a cub scout troop?

Vlad the Arkela.

What's the most musical fish?

A piano tuna.

A conjurer was working on a cruise ship with his pet parrot. All through his act the parrot would squawk, 'It's up his sleeve!' or 'It's in his pocket!'

A fortnight into the voyage the ship hit a rock and sank. In the morning all there was to be seen in the vast ocean was the conjurer and his parrot, clinging to a piece of wreckage.

After three hours the parrot looked at the conjurer and said, 'Alright, I give up. What have you done with the ship?'

Why wouldn't they let the architect build a skyscraper?

There were too many floors in his design.

Why was the pirate good at boxing?

He had a great left hook.

Did you hear about the contortionist who lost his job and fell on hard times?

He just couldn't make ends meet.

What do you call a decomposing whale?

Mouldy Dick.

Patient: Doctor, I've just come out in spots, like cherries on a cake.

Doctor: Ah, you must have analogy.

Patient: Doctor, I keep thinking I'm a dog.

Doctor: Well, do you chase balls in the park?

Patient: No, of course not! I'm not allowed off the lead in the park.

Why are beavers regularly employed in data analysis?

They're great with log rhythms.

What do you call a Grammy-winning Canadian pop star who likes building dams?"

Justin Beaver.

What do you call a German beaver with his own pottery wheel?

Potsdam.

What do you call an opera-loving German beaver who likes building dams on ladders?

Götterdämmerung.

What do beavers think of plasticized wooden decking?

Nothing. They just ignaw it.

How many tickles does it take to make an octopus laugh?

Ten tickles.

My dog is a genius at mathematics. I asked her, 'What's four minus four?'

She said nothing.

Visitor: Excuse me, what ward is Mr Smith in?

Nurse: The man run over by a steamroller?
Wards 5, 6 and 7.

How much energy does it take to electrocute someone?
One killer-Watt.

If you go into the toilet American and come out of the toilet American, what are you while you're in the toilet?
European!

Teacher: Does anyone know what flatulence is?
Lucy: It's the ambulance they take you to hospital in if you've been run over by a steam-roller.

Child: Mummy, last night I saw the baby-sitter kissing a strange man in our living room.

Mum: What?!

Tommy: April Fool! ... it was only Daddy.

What goes,
'I'm dreaming of a —
KABOOM!!!'

Bang Crosby.

Judge: You shoplifted a tin of tomatoes, so I sentence you to four weeks in prison, one for each tomato.

Defendant's wife: Don't forget he also stole a tin of peas, your honour.

Why do pirates only get dangerous from the age of ten?
Because afore that they be nine.

What do you call pain-free yoghurts?

Yogs.

Wayne: How was your fortnight in Wales?

Wesley: Not bad. It only rained twice – once for seven days and the second time for a week.

My dog is a descriptive genius. I asked her what kind of sound you'd get if you lit a fire with a gallon of kerosene? She said, 'Woof!'

A lecturer of Ancient Greek took his trousers to be mended. 'Euripedes?' asked the tailor. **'Yes,' replied the lecturer. 'Eumenides?'**

What's white, has one horn and delivers milk?

A milk lorry.

What do you get if you cross an inflatable trampoline with a legendary pop diva?

A Beyoncé Castle

What does the King call his Christmas broadcast?

The One Show.

Footballer: Would you send me off if I said you were a useless referee?

Referee: Yes.

Footballer: But you couldn't send me off for thinking it?

Referee: No.

Footballer: Right then, I think you're a useless referee.

A gravel lorry played a concrete lorry at football.

The gravel won on aggregate.

Wayne: I backed a horse in the two o'clock at Kempton at ten to one.

Wesley: What happened?

Wayne: It came in at half-past four.

Teacher: Who knows what a juggernaut is?

Sally: Is it an empty beer glass, miss?

Wayne: I'm not feeling very well.
Wesley: Well you should take those mittens off.

Wayne: I had a text the other day and it said 'IDK'. What does that mean?

Amy: I Don't Know.

Wayne: No, neither did I.

Wayne: I'm going to change my bank.
Wesley: Why's that?
Wayne: I went in yesterday and asked the lady if she'd check my balance, and she pushed me over!

Wayne and Wesley were fishing when the bailiff arrived. As soon as he saw him, Wayne threw his rod down and started running as fast as he could. The bailiff gave chase, and after a ten-minute pursuit Wayne stopped running and showed the bailiff his fishing licence.
'Why did you run away if you've got a licence?'
asked the bailiff.
'I might have a licence,' said Wayne, 'but Wesley hasn't.'

A vicar was walking down the street when he saw a little girl trying to reach a high-up knocker on a front door. 'Let me help,' he said, and knocked on the door. 'Now, is there anything else I can do?'
'Yes,' said the girl. 'Now we run like hell!'

Patient: I'm having trouble breathing.
Doctor: Don't worry, I'll soon stop that.

Why do bears hibernate for so long?

Would you like to go in and wake one up?

Dad: What's all this arguing about?

Kids: We all want to play with the same toy.

Dad: Right, whoever never talks back to Mum and obeys her instantly can have it first.

Kids: OK, Dad, you can have it.

Patient: Are these tablets addictive?

Doctor: Definitely not. I've been taking them myself for years.

Patient: I keep having this awful dream. I'm in front of a door with writing on it, and I push and I push and I push but it won't open.
Doctor: What does the writing say?
Patient: 'Pull'.

What happened to the man who beat his bed to death?

He was charged with matricide.

What's the difference between a cat and a comma?
One has the paws before the claws, and the other has the clause before the pause.

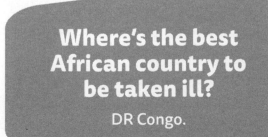

Where's the best African country to be taken ill?

DR Congo.

What did the policeman say when he cut himself shaving?

I'm nicked!

Son: What's the point of me learning a trade? There aren't any jobs.
Dad: Yes, but at least then we'd know what work you were out of.

Interviewer: There are two things we value at this company – honesty and cleanliness. So, first question: did you wipe your feet on the doormat on the way in?
Candidate: Yes, I certainly did.
Interviewer: That's interesting, because we haven't got a doormat.

Ollie was watching his mum put on face cream. 'What's that for?' he asked.
'It's to make me look beautiful,' she told him.
After a couple of minutes she started to wipe it off.
'Giving up already...?'

Mum: How would you describe me?

Dad: ABCDEFGHIJK.

Mum: What do you mean?

Dad: Adorable, beautiful, cute, delightful, elegant, funny, graceful, helpful, intelligent.

Mum: What about JK?

Dad: Just Kidding.

What's brown, hairy, wears sunglasses and carries a stethoscope?

A coconut disguised as a doctor.

Doctor: I'd advise you to give up drinking and smoking.

Patient: At my age, surely it's too late.

Doctor: It's never too late.

Patient: Well in that case there's no rush, is there?

My boss asked me why I only get sick on work days. I said it must be my weekend immune system.

How many jugglers does it take to change a lightbulb?

One. But you'll need three lightbulbs.

How many folk singers does it take to change a lightbulb?

Five. One to change it and four to sing about how good the old one was.

What do you call a woman who burns down banks?
Bernadette.

How many teenagers does it take to change a lightbulb?

46. One to change it, one to film it for TikTok and 44 to spend five hours talking about how EPIC it was.

Why did the crew of the *Starship Enterprise* eject a beaver into deep space?

They caught it gnawing the captain's log.

Amy: My husband's got hundreds of people under him where he works.

Lauren: Your husband? Never!

Amy: It's true, he's a gardener at the local cemetery.

Wayne: You look puzzled, Wesley.

Wesley: I was just wondering, how come whenever I ring a wrong number it's never engaged?

Terrible golfer: What do you think of my game?

Caddy: I think I prefer golf.

First person in pub: Have you seen that ridiculous-looking girl dancing over there?

Second person: Do you mind, that's my *son*.

First person: I'm so sorry, I didn't realize you were his father.

Second person: I'm his *mother*!

Where do birds drink coffee?

In a nest-café.

Bertha: Why do you call your enormous knickers 'harvest festivals'?

Amy: Because all is safely gathered in.

Wayne: What's your favourite time of the day?

Wesley: 6:30 – it wins hands down.

What's a cannibal's favourite meal?

Snake and pygmy pie.

Wayne: I dropped my watch last night.
Wesley: Did it break?
Wayne: No, luckily it fell on its hands.

Two men who overdosed on curry powder for a dare are now in hospital. One's in a korma and the other's got a dodgy tikka.

Teacher: How many degrees in a circle?
Ollie: It depends, sir.
Teacher: What on?
Ollie: Do you want the answer in Fahrenheit or Celsius?

What do you call a useless, incontinent ostrich?

A dire rhea.

Why did the world's first dating agency for chickens go bust?

They couldn't make hens meet!

Dad: Hello, love. Sorry I'm away at this business conference. Are you missing me?
Mum: Yes and no.
Dad: What do you mean?
Mum: Well, I'm so miserable it's almost as if you're still here.

Footballer: Why have you given a penalty, ref?
Referee: You just burped right into my face.
Footballer: Well, that should only be a freak hic.

What guard has one hundred legs?

A sentry-pede!

Wayne: My brother went to pieces when he went to jail.
Wesley: How do you mean?
Wayne: He wouldn't stop jabbering, took all his clothes off and broke all the furniture.
We haven't played Monopoly since!

What do you call a chicken that thinks it's an ancient warrior?

Attila the Hen.

What's purple, 5,000 miles long and full of pips?
The grape wall of China.

Norman went mountain climbing, his rope broke and he ended up clinging to the cliff face by a thin branch. 'Is there anybody up there who can help me, anybody!' he shouted desperately.

Suddenly a voice spoke: 'NORMAN, THIS IS GOD. LET GO OF THE BRANCH AND I WILL SEE YOU LAND SAFELY.'

Norman was silent for a few seconds, and then said, 'Is there anybody else up there...?'

Where do ghosts go for a night out at Christmas?

The phantomime.

What does Professor Dumbledore put on his hanky when he's got a cold?

Albus Oil!

What do you call a bear who leans on her paws?
Pauline.

What do you call a bear who refuses to lean on her paws?
Noeline.

Wesley: Last week I fell in front of a moving train.

Wayne: How did you survive that?

Wesley: It was going backwards.

Two hikers are walking along a trail in the mountains. All of a sudden, the gravel in front of the first hiker says, 'Your walking boots are really dirty, you should clean them.' Then, a little further on, some pebbles on the track say to her, 'You've got a really stupid walk, and you're scuffing your feet.'

The first hiker is really confused by this and turns to her friend who says, 'Don't worry, that happens to everyone – it's just a critical path...'

Wayne: I'd like a room for the night, please.

Hotel owner: I'm sorry, sir, we're full up.

Wayne: I bet if the president turned up wanting a room, you'd find one for him.

Hotel owner: Yes, I suppose we would.

Wayne: Well, he's not coming – I'll have his room.

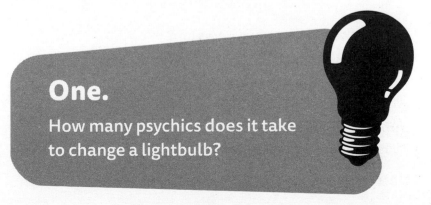

One.
How many psychics does it take to change a lightbulb?

What has a bottom at the top?
Your legs.

What do you call a teacher with no arms, no legs and no body?
The head.

When do cannibals leave the table?
After everyone's eaten.

Lauren: Times have changed, haven't they?

Lucy: I'll say. My kids have got so many expensive gadgets in their bedrooms, when they're naughty I have to send them to *my* room.

Doctor: I've got some bad news and some good news.
Patient: Give me the bad news first.
Doctor: You're suffering from three different deadly diseases.
Patient: And the good news?
Doctor: I know how to cure two of them.

Wayne: I went to the doctor yesterday and he told me I had one buttock longer than the other.

Wesley: What a down right cheek!

Customer: A pint of bitter and a packet of helicopter crisps.

Barman: I'm sorry, we've only got plane crisps.

When beavers travel around the UK which hotel chain do they like to stay in?

Travel Lodge.

Patient: I can't stop gloating all the time.

Doctor: Have this cream, and *don't* rub it in.

Wayne: I got sacked from my job at the Samaritans because of a man who rang up saying he was lying on the railway track waiting for a train.

Wesley: Why?

Wayne: Apparently, 'Remain calm and stay on the line' was the wrong thing to say.

Wesley: My son was born on St George's Day, so we called him George.

Wayne: That's funny, my son was born on St Patrick's Day, so we called him Patrick.

Harold: That's funny, that's exactly what we did with my son Pancake.

Why did the farmer feed his pigs one day and starve them the next?
He was trying to produce streaky bacon.

I finally got round to watching that documentary on clocks. It was about time.

Two men and a woman went for a job as an assassin with the CIA.

The first man was given a gun and told to go into a room and shoot the person sitting on the chair. He went in and came straight out again. 'That's my wife in there,' he said, 'I can't kill her.' So he was told he'd failed the test.

The second man was told the same thing, went into the room and came out after a minute. 'It was my wife,' he said, 'I just couldn't bring myself to pull the trigger.' He failed.

Finally the woman went in. She was in for five minutes, during which there was a loud commotion from the room. She finally came out breathless and dishevelled. 'You might have told me my husband was going to be in there,' she panted. 'And the stupid gun was full of blanks, so I had to beat him to death with the chair.'

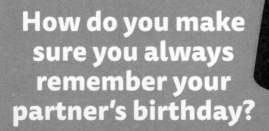

How do you make sure you always remember your partner's birthday?

Forget it once.

Sally: I named my dogs Rolex and Casio. I've always wanted watchdogs.

Wayne: I see those two lavatory attendants got married.

Wesley: Yes, but I think it's just a marriage of convenience.

Patient: What's that man doing hanging from your ceiling?

Psychiatrist: Oh, he's another patient – he thinks he's a light bulb.

Patient: Can't you cure him?

Psychiatrist: I could, but then I'd have to work in the dark.

What's the stupidest animal in the jungle?

The penguin.

Knock, knock.

Who's there?

Nobel.

Nobel who?

No bell. That's why I knocked.

What do you call the home of a Dutch beaver?
Amsterdam.

_____

Why did Count Vlad frighten off the interior designers in his local village?
He asked them up to the castle for a re-vamp.

_____

First robot: Have you got any brothers?
Second robot: No, just transistors.

What do you call the home of a Dutch beaver that's gone to rack and ruin?

Rotterdam

Cake Shop Customer: Is that a doughnut or a meringue?
Baker: No, you're right. It's a doughnut.

Dad: What's the difference between a terrorist and your Mum?

Son: I don't know.

Dad: You can negotiate with a terrorist.

Son: I'm not sure I want to use this glue stick.

Dad: Why not?

Son: It says, 'To use, take off the top and push up bottom.'

A man went parachuting for the first time. The instructor told him, 'Count to five and pull on the main chute; if that doesn't open, count to ten and pull on the reserve chute. Then you'll float slowly down to the ground and our truck will be there to drive you back to the airfield.'

The man jumped out, pulled the main chute – nothing happened. He pulled the reserve chute – nothing happened. He looked down at the fast-approaching ground and thought to himself: 'I bet that truck won't be there to pick me up either.'

Dentist: I've got some good news and some bad news. The good news is that your teeth are fine.

Patient: What's the bad news?

Dentist: All your gums have got to come out.

What do you give a stressed-out elephant?

Trunkquilisers!

Customer: I'd like to return this piano stool.

Music shop assistant: What's wrong with it?

Customer: I can't get a note out of it!

What's invisible and makes funny clucking noises around your house?

A poultrygeist.

A man went into a pub feeling low and said to the barmaid, 'A pint, a pie and a few kind words, please.' The barmaid poured him a pint and slapped a pie in front of him without saying anything. 'What about the few kind words?' he pleaded. 'Don't eat the pie.'

What do you get if you cross a pitbull with a St Bernard?

A dog that bites your leg off then gives you a drink of brandy.

Billy: My Mum and Dad bought me these rollerblades from the Pound Shop

Bobby: Cheapskates.

What's a beaver's *least* favourite film?

The Dam Busters.

Diner: What goes best with a jacket potato?
Waiter: I'd recommend *button* mushrooms and *thai* noodles.

Maths teacher: Who knows what a ratio is?

Ollie: He's a sailor, sir.

Teacher: What do you mean, a sailor?

Ollie: A ratio Nelson.

After a late night Wayne and Wesley realized they'd missed the last bus back to Wolverhampton. As they were passing the bus depot, Wayne suggested nipping in and 'borrowing' a bus to get them home.

Wesley kept lookout, and after half an hour and much revving of engines, Wayne finally emerged at the wheel of a double-decker.

'What took you so long?' asked Wesley.

'It wasn't my fault,' said Wayne, 'all the Wolverhampton buses were at the back.'

What do you get if you cross the Atlantic with an accountant?

A Boring 747.

What can a whole onion do that half an onion can't?

Look round!

Wayne: Cornet, please.

Ice cream man: Hundreds and thousands?

Wayne: No, just one.

Homes are too expensive in my area so I had to move into my friend's bouncy castle.

The rent's really high, but that's mostly due to inflation.

Wayne: Our working men's club is looking for a treasurer.
Wesley: But I thought you hired one last month?
Wayne: That's the one we're looking for...

How does an alien count to forty-six?

On its fingers.

Did you hear about the snake who worked for the government?

He was a civil serpent.

Who drives round the West Country in a camper van?

Tess of the Dormobiles.

Teacher: What's wrong with your peas, Ollie?

Ollie: They're too hard, sir.

Teacher: Let me try some off your plate ... hmm, they don't seem *that* hard.

Ollie: No, but I've been chewing those for the last ten minutes.

Ollie: Dad, the gas cooker's just gone out.

Dad: Well, relight it then.

Ollie: I can't, it went out through the ceiling.

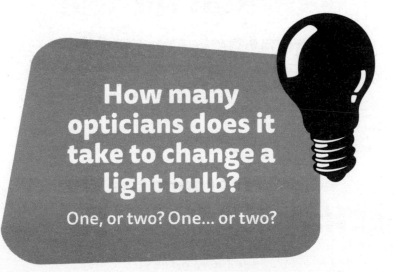

How many opticians does it take to change a light bulb?

One, or two? One... or two?

Teacher: Who knows what 'centimetre' means?

Jane: When my Gran arrived on the train, Dad was centimetre.

Wesley: This car you sold me is terrible. I thought you said it had one careful owner.

Salesman: I didn't say *all* its owners were careful.

Where do vampires go for a little side hustle?

Only Fangs.com

What did Delaware?

Her New Jersey!

Wesley: My parrot lays square eggs.
Wayne: Can it talk?
Wesley: It can only say one word – 'Ouch!'

Why did the ant elope?

No one gnu.

What's a boxer's favourite part of a joke?
The denouement.*

What did the cheese say to the mirror?

Halloumi!

* were you expecting a better *punch*line?

I changed a lightbulb, answered a knock at the door, crossed the road and walked into a bar.

Then I realised I was living in a joke.

A man was walking on a beach when he found an old lamp. He gave it a rub and, of course, a genie appeared, promising to grant him one wish (he was a mean genie). 'Well, I've got relatives in Canada, but I hate flying. Please build me a bridge between England and Canada so I can visit them more often.'

The genie laughed. 'I'm sorry, that's impossible, even for me. The materials, construction problems, shipping lanes, it's out of the question. Have another wish.'

'Fair enough,' said the man. 'Well, I love football and it's always been my wish to see England win the World Cup.'

The genie thought for a minute then asked, 'How many lanes do you want on this bridge?'

Vegans think that people who sell meat are disgusting; but people who sell fruit and veg are grocer.

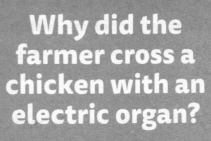

Why did the farmer cross a chicken with an electric organ?

So he could have Hammond eggs.

What happened to the couple who met in a revolving door?

They've been going round together for ages.

Optician: You need glasses.
Patient: How do you know without examining me?
Optician: It was something about the way you came in through the window.

What's a golfer's favourite deodorant?

Links!

A man was returning to his seat in the theatre after a 'comfort break'.

'Excuse me,' he said to the lady by the aisle.

'Did I step on your foot when I went out?'

'Yes, you did,' said the lady.

'Oh good, that means I'm in the right row.'

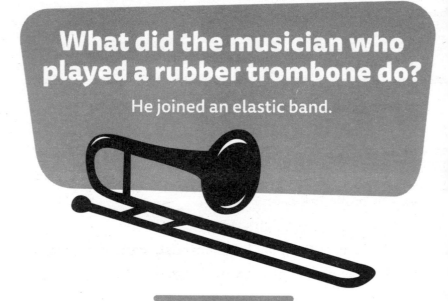

What did the musician who played a rubber trombone do?

He joined an elastic band.

What was the most amazing thing they discovered when they found the wreck of the *Titanic*?

After over a hundred years, the swimming pool was still full.

How can you tell when witches are carrying a time bomb?

You can hear their brooms tick.

A traffic policeman stopped a car that was trundling slowly along the M25 and asked him, 'Why are you going so slowly, sir? You're holding up traffic.'

'Well,' replied the motorist, 'the signs say "25".'

'But that's just the road number, not the speed limit,' said the copper. Then he noticed that a woman in the back seat was trembling all over.

'Is your passenger all right, sir?'

'Don't worry, officer,' said the motorist, 'my wife's always like that when we come off the A127.'

What's the difference between Joan of Arc and Noah's Ark?

Joan of Arc was Maid of Orleans and Noah's Ark was made of wood.

Knock, knock

Who's there?

Spell.

Spell who?

Okay, fine. W-H-O.

Why does Rudolf have a red nose and all the other reindeer have brown ones?
Rudolf's the only one whose brakes work.

What lives in America, has four eyes and runs all day long?
The Mississippi.

Amy (on phone): Hello Wayne, the car won't start, the engine's damp.

Wayne: How do you know it's damp?

Amy: Because I've driven into the canal.

My friend wants to live to the age of 120 and told me he'd found a special white serum that will help him achieve this *amazing* goal.
I looked at the container in his fridge.
I said, 'I don't want to disappoint you, but it's the milk that has the Long Life...'

A footballer was getting out of his Bentley when another car zoomed past and ripped the car door clean off. When the police arrived the footballer was still moaning about the damage to his car.

The policeman said, 'Sir, never mind your precious car, don't you realise your left arm was torn off in the accident?'

The footballer looked at the stump where his arm used to be and yelled, 'Nooooooooooo! My Rolex!'

What is a teacup?

Nineteen sizes up on an A-cup.

I went for a job as a rubbish collector, but they gave me no training at all.

They said I could pick it up as I go along.

A man was getting nothing done at work, as his workstation was cluttered with little figurines – Marilyn Monroe, Che Guevara, Madonna, Gandhi, etc.

A colleague walked past and said, 'You've got an IT problem.'

'What do you mean?' asked the man.

'You've got too many icons on your desktop.'

Doctor: Stop worrying about your health. You'll live to be eighty.
Patient: I am eighty!
Doctor: What did I tell you!

Which Canadian city do all beavers try and avoid?

Ottawa

My partner told me I had problems expressing my emotions.

I can't say I'm surprised.

Where do hobbits buy their furniture?

Hobitat.

Patient: Doctor, I think I'm a clock.

Doctor: Are you winding me up?

Why did the man try to gatecrash a party dressed as a pirate and a shepherd?

He was going to get in by hook or by crook!

A young sea cadet was being tested by an examiner.

Examiner: Suppose you're at sea and a storm comes up?

Cadet: I'd toss out an anchor.

Examiner: And what if another storm came in?

Cadet: I'd toss out another anchor.

Examiner: But what if an even bigger storm arose?

Cadet: I'd toss out another anchor.

Examiner: Ah, but tell me – where are you getting all your anchors from?

Cadet: The same place you're getting your storms.

Interviewer: If you got the job as zoo keeper, what steps would you take if the lions escaped?

Wayne: Great big ones!

Why do melons get upset when they're crossed with cauliflowers?

It makes them melon-colly.

How many polite Parisians does it take to change a lightbulb?

Either of them.

What happened when the missionary met the cannibal?

He gave him his first taste of religion.

Patient: Doctor, I think I'm a famous psychoanalyst.

Doctor: How long has this been going on?

Patient: Ever since I was Jung.

Wesley: I'm fed up with my wife.

Wayne: Why?

Wesley: She texted me last night to say she was in Casualty. I watched the whole episode and never saw her.

Why did the computer technician's toaster stop working?

He'd disabled pop-ups.

Wayne: Why are you buying condensed milk?

Wesley: Well, I've only got a small fridge.

Patient: Dr Finlay, whenever I eat chocolate and coconut it gives me stomach ache.

Dr Finlay: Och, it's boun' tae.

A young policeman came off his first late shift and was surprised to be given a bag of blue crystals by his boss.

'What's this?' he asked.

'It's the copper nitrate.'

Why do ants never get ill?

They have anty bodies.

How do you get a one-armed idiot out of a tree?

Give him a wave.

Mum: We've been married twenty years – how old do you think I look? Be honest!

Dad: Well, from your skin I'd say twenty-eight, from your hair, twenty-five, from your figure, twenty-nine.

Mum: Oh, what a lovely thing to say.

Dad: Hang on, I haven't finished adding it up yet.

'Doctor, I keep seeing frogs before my eyes.'
'Don't worry, it's just a hoptical illusion.'

'Doctor, I keep thinking I'm a small bucket.'
'You do look a little pale.'

'Whenever someone says, "I don't believe in coincidences," I say, "Oh my God, me neither!"'

Where do farmers buy their cows?

From a cattle-ogue.

Wayne: My wife bet me I couldn't make a car out of spaghetti.

Wesley: What happened?

Wayne: Well, you should have seen her face when I drove pasta.

Wayne: My wife said she wanted me to buy her something that will go from 0 to 200 in a few seconds.

Wesley: That sounds expensive, what have you bought her?

Wayne: A set of bathroom scales.

First scientist: I've just discovered a faster-than-light particle.

Second scientist: I bet you didn't see that coming.

What did Columbus ask the shipwright when he went to buy a new ship?
How many miles to the galleon does it do?

First idiot: Christmas Day is going to be on a Friday this year.
Second idiot: Let's hope it's not the 13th then!

Why was the short-sighted magician banned by the Magic Circle?

He tried to pull a rabbi out of a hat.

Two men were on a building site, one weedy and little, one big and strong. The little guy said, 'I bet you twenty quid I can push something to the end of the yard in my wheelbarrow and you won't be able to push the same thing back.'

'You're on,' replied the big guy.

'Right,' said the weed, 'jump in...'

What happened when there was an explosion in a French cheese factory?
All that was left was de brie.

What was the bug doing in the computer?
Looking for a byte to eat.

Wayne: I've just auditioned for *Snow White and the Seven Dwarfs*.

Wesley: Did you get the part?

Wayne: I don't know, but I'm on the short list.

Patient: Doctor, I've been coughing for a month and nothing you've done has helped.

Doctor: Right, I'm going to give you a massive dose of laxative.

Patient: Will that cure my cough?

Doctor: Put it this way, you won't dare to.

Wayne: I've been thinking about rising sea levels.

Wesley: What about them?

Wayne: Well, just think how much higher it would be if there weren't any sponges in the sea.

A man walks into a bar.

So that's him eliminated from the High Jump competition.

Wayne: I had to get up really early this morning and answer the door in my pyjamas.

Wesley: Why on earth have you got a door in your pyjamas?

Which nationality always does well in giant vegetable competitions?

The Swedes.

Wesley and Wayne were on a plane to New York when the captain came on the intercom. 'I'm afraid one of our four engines has failed, there's no danger, but we will be an hour late arriving in New York.'

Half an hour later he came on again: 'Very sorry, but a second engine has failed. Still no problem, but we will be two hours late in New York.'

An hour further on the captain spoke again: 'Please don't worry, the third engine has failed. We'll be all right, but we will be three hours late in New York.'

At this Wesley turned to Wayne and said, 'Let's hope the fourth engine doesn't fail, or we'll be up here all night!'

What did the amorous beaver say to his new mate?

'I love you like no otter.'

Wayne: I'm sorry, Wesley, I've just run over your cat. Can I replace it?

Wesley: That depends how good you are at catching mice.

What do you call a stupid Viking?

The pillage idiot.

Woman: Doctor, my husband thinks he's a parachute.

Doctor: Tell him to drop in and see me.

Wesley: I bought a rocket salad drizzled with olive oil.

Wayne: Was it nice?

Wesley: I don't know, it went off before I could eat it.

Dinner guest: Why is your dog looking at me like that?

Host: Don't worry, he just doesn't like you using his plate.

What happened to the man with five legs?

His trousers fit him like a glove.

Wayne: A pile of books fell on my head yesterday.
Wesley: You ought to sue someone.
Wayne: No, I've only got my shelf to blame.

Wayne: I've just had a man from Eastern Europe clean my house. It took him four hours to hoover the carpets.
Wesley: It sounds like he was a Slovak.

Wesley: This furniture goes back to Louis the Fourteenth.

Wayne: Really?

Wesley: Yes, unless we pay Louis by the Thirteenth.

Wayne: Has your tooth stopped hurting yet?

Wesley: I don't know, the dentist kept it.

Why did Taylor Swift's management get rid of her large ant entourage...?

They were sycophants

A man answered a knock on the door to find a snail on the doorstep. He picked up the snail and threw it as far as he could.

Two years later he answered another knock on the door and there was a snail on the doorstep again. The snail said, 'Why did you do that?'

When are children the most biased?

At Christmas – it's bias this, bias that...

A community artist was commissioned to take *culture* to the people.

So... he played some Vivaldi in Aldi.
He painted a fresco in Tesco.
He sketched a star in Spar.
But in Lidl ... he was arrested for gross indecency.

What do you never hear in school?

The letter H.

Policeman: Did you see the vehicle that hit you?

Man: No, but I know it was my mother-in-law driving – I'd recognise that laugh anywhere.

What happened to the man who tried to pick up too many colanders full of seafood?

He strained his muscles!

Wayne: Did you sign up for that online account?

Wesley: No, it wouldn't let me. It kept asking me to choose a password with eight characters including a number.

Wayne: So what was the problem?

Wesley: Well, no matter how many times I typed in 'Snow White and the Seven Dwarfs' it wouldn't accept it.

I had a weird dream that I weighed less than a hundredth of a gram.

I was like, 'Omg!'

Wayne: The doctor put me on a diet of coconuts and bananas.

Wesley: Have you lost much weight?

Wayne: No, but you should see me climb a tree.

Patient: Doctor, can you give me anything for my halitosis?

Doctor: Take a spoonful of horse manure twice a day.

Patient: Will that cure it?

Doctor: No, but it'll take the edge off the smell.

What's red and bad for your teeth?

A brick.

How many sociologists does it take to change a light bulb?

The light bulb is fine – it's the system that has to change.

Wayne and Wesley went into a pub and started playing pool. After an hour neither had potted a ball.

'Wayne,' said Wesley, 'let's see what happens if we take that wooden frame off...'

I decided to put my vacuum cleaner on eBay.

All it was doing was gathering dust.

Two nuns are driving down a narrow country lane when they meet a drunk weaving across the road in front of them. They drive right up to him, rev the engine, toot the horn, but he won't move out of the way.

Then one nun has an idea. 'Sister Maria, why don't you show him your cross.'

So Sister Maria wound down the window and shouted, 'Get out of the flaming way, you drunken old reprobate!'

I had a weird dream that the band Orchestral Manoeuvres in the Dark changed their name to Orchestral Manoeuvres in the Garden.

I was like, 'OMG!'

Teacher: Who knows what a goblet is?

Jane: Is it a baby turkey?

Why did the idiot give up fish-farming?

His tractor kept getting stuck in the river.

A dad was washing his car with his son.

Son: Why can't you use a sponge like everybody else?

Two Aussie blokes are hiking in the Australian outback when one is bitten on the bum by a rattlesnake. Luckily the other has a signal on his mobile phone, and he calls for the flying doctor.

'Listen,' says the doctor, 'I can't get to you for an hour – if you don't suck the poison out in the next ten minutes your friend will die.'

'What did he say?' asks the victim.

'Mate, he says you're going to die.'

Did you know the Lone Ranger has a cousin in a London park who's a florist?

He's the Hyde Ranger.

A Yorkshireman's wife died and he asked the stonemason to put a simple inscription on her headstone: 'She was thine'. But when he went to inspect the work, it said, 'She was thin'.

'You daft beggar, you've missed off the "e",' he complained. The stonemason said he'd put it right for the next day.

Sure enough, when the man returned the next day the stone read: 'Ee, She was thin'.

Wayne: I worry that you only want to marry me because my father left me a fortune.

Amy: Don't be silly. I'd want to marry you whoever left you a fortune.

What do you call an elephant that nobody has time for?

It's irrelevant.

My wife gets really angry when I tell her she has no sense of direction.

One day she snapped. She stormed upstairs, packed her bags and right ...

I wrote a great book on how to build a new staircase at home.

It was a step-by-step guide.

... Then I wrote a book on how to build two large Russian ecosystems.

That was a steppe-by-steppe guide.

... Then I asked the Golden State Warriors' greatest basketball player to write his autobiography.

It was a Steph-by-Steph guide.

Teacher: What's a bacteria?

Ollie: The rear door to a cafeteria.

Wayne: I met my wife in a nightclub.

Wesley: What was the first thing you said to her?

Wayne: I said, 'I thought you were at home looking after the kids.'

Wayne: I'm packing in my job as a human cannonball.

Wesley: That's a shame – where are they going to find someone of your calibre?

What did the farmer say to the cow on his roof?

Get off my roof!

Knock, knock.
Who's there?
Déjàv
Déjàv who?
Knock, knock.

What's the best way to keep milk from going off?

Leave it in the cow.

Amy: Why do you call your daughter 'Nature'?
Lauren: Because she abhors a vacuum.

Wayne: Gavin died last week, he had terrible heartburn and swallowed too much medicine.

Wesley: You mean Gav is gone?

Why did the hipster beaver abandon his lodge on the river?

He said it was too main-stream.

Why did Courtney Cox?

Because Lisa Kudrow.

Customer: I'd like to buy a watch, please.
Jeweller: Certainly, sir, analogue?
Customer: No, just a watch.

Who killed Dracula with a sausage roll?

Buffet the vampire-slayer.

Wayne: I was so unpopular at school they used to call me 'Batteries'.
Wesley: Why?
Wayne: Because I was never included in anything.

What do you call a Flintstones-themed party in the United Arab Emirates?

The Abu Dhabi do.

My son hated it when I put him on the My Little Pony carousel ride at the fairground.

But he eventually came round.

Why does a flamingo lift one foot off the floor?

Because if it lifted both feet it would fall over.

Impatient Diner: Excuse me, I've been waiting here for half an hour, it's a disgrace!
Waiter: How do you think I feel, I've been waiting here for six years!

Coroner: Do you remember your husband's last words?
Widow: Yes, he said, how on earth can the butcher make any money selling meat this cheap?

Wayne: What's the best thing about Switzerland?

Wesley: Well, the flag is a big plus ...

A man was walking through his local park when he saw two council workers. One would dig a hole, move on a few feet, dig another one, and so on. The other was following him, filling in all the holes he'd dug.

The man was furious. He stormed up to the workers, saying, 'I'm going to write to the council, all this digging holes and filling them in again, it's a disgrace.'

'Hang on,' said the filler-in. 'It's not our fault that Charlie's off sick.'

'Who's Charlie?' asked the man.

'He's the bloke who plants the trees.'

What was the score when The Sadler's Wells Ballet played the Bolshoi Ballet at football yesterday.

It ended in a 2–2.

How do you think the unthinkable?

With an itheberg.

Do zombies like being dead?

Of corpse they do.

Teacher: Complete the saying, 'Those who live by the sword...'

Ollie: Get shot by those who live by the gun.

———

Hetty: I showed my doctor a rash on my chest yesterday and he was all embarrassed and uncomfortable.

Hattie: That's very unprofessional, what did he say?

Hetty: He told me to make an appointment like everyone else and said he was never going to shop in Aldi again.

———

What is a beaver's all-time favourite movie?

Reservoir Logs.

What happens to ducklings when they grow up?

They grow down!

Wayne: I've got a joke, I might have told you it before.

Wesley: Is it a funny one?

Wayne: Oh yes.

Wesley: Then you haven't.

What did the pirate say on his eightieth birthday?

Aye, Matey!

Wayne: Have you heard of that new website for learning ventriloquism?

Wesley: What's the address?

Wayne: Guggle-yew, Guggle-yew, Guggle-yew, dot ...

Patient: How was that, doc?

Doctor: Very impressive, but I said I wanted to hear your *heart*?

Amy: When I grow up, do you think my name will be in lights in theatres across the country?

Lauren: Only if you change your name to 'Emergency Exit'.

Teacher: Which month has twenty-eight days?

Billy: All of them, sir.

Time flies like
an arrow
Fruit flies like
a banana.

What do you get if
you cross an elk with
an Easter egg?
Chocolate moose.

Teacher: What sort of bird is a macaw?

Billy: Is it a Scottish crow, miss?

What do you get if you cross a hyena with a man-eating tiger?
I don't know.
Neither do I, but if it laughs you'd better join in.

What do you call someone who lends tools to his neighbour?

A saw loser.

Wayne: Where are you off to?

Wesley: To a surprise party for Amy – weren't you invited?

Wayne: No, but I'll come anyway – it'll be an even bigger surprise.

Wayne: Last night someone painted 'NGAB' on my car.

Wesley: That's bang out of order, that is.

Rav: I really hate it when my aunties and grannies come up to me at weddings and say, 'You're next!'

Jas: Well, you should do the same to them at funerals.

Where do frogs fly their flags?

On tadpoles.

A treason plot has been uncovered among a group of blackcurrants.

The purple traitors have been arrested.

What happened to the Eskimo who sat on the ice all day?

He got Polaroids.

Pub landlord: I had to throw out that Spanish actor who played the baddie in *Skyfall* the other day.

Wayne: Javier Bardem?

Publican: No, he can come back when he sobers up.

Son: What's inside an acorn?

Dad: In a nutshell... it's an oak tree.

Wayne: I've just had a letter from a Lancashire drag artist.

Wesley: How do you work that out?

Wayne: Well, he had a Wigan address.

Wayne: My Mum and Dad were called Pearl and Dean.

Wesley: Don't you mean your Ma and Pa-pa-pa-pa-pa-pa-pa-pa-pa-pa-pa?

Woman: Doctor, my son thinks he's a chicken.

Doctor: Why haven't you brought him in, I'm sure I can do something.

Woman: Yes, but we need the eggs.

Railway inspector: What would you do if you realized two trains were heading towards each other on the same line?

Signalman: I'd change the points to divert one of them.

Inspector: And if the points were broken?

Signalman: I'd shut both signals to red.

Inspector: And if the signals failed?

Signalman: I'd flag them down with my shirt.

Inspector: And if it was at night?

Signalman: I'd flag them down with my lamp.

Inspector: And if your lamp was out of batteries?

Signalman: I'd go and fetch my brother, Charlie.

Inspector: Why would you fetch your brother?

Signalman: Well, he's never seen a train crash before.

What dog has no head?
A King Charles the First spaniel.

How long does it take to buy a Mexican dog?
Chihuahuas.

What do clouds wear under their trousers?

Thunderpants!

My wife left me because of my addiction to Citizen's Band radio. She said: 'It's over!'

I said: 'It's what? Over.'

What do you call a man stuck between two buildings?

Ali.

What's a Freudian slip?

It's when you say one thing and mean a mother.

What did Sigmund Freud say came between fear and sex?

Funf.

The woman who invented auto-correct is getting married.

Her Wednesday is at the chirp on satellite.

What did astronaut Neil Armstrong say to chef Heston Blumenthal when he took a bag of chips onto Brighton pier?

'Heston, the seagulls have landed!'

What did Jay-Z call his wife before they got married?

Feyoncé!

How did Edison invent electric lighting?

He had a lightbulb moment.

Wayne: I'm fed up of being told I have to change my password.
Wesley: It's a pain, isn't it?
Wayne: Yes, I've had to rename my dog four times now. He objects to being called Fido%47!

Why is six o'clock in the morning like a pig's tail?
Because it's twirly.

What's the difference between jam and marmalade?

You can't get stuck in a traffic marmalade.

Lawyer: My client will never get justice! Half of the judges in this country are crooks.
Judge: You must withdraw that remark.
Lawyer: Very well, my lord. Half of the judges in this country are *not* crooks.

What do you call a caveman with no sense of direction?

A meanderthal!

Wesley: It's taken me ages, but I've made a belt out of old watches.
Wayne: That sounds like a waist of time.

How do snails keep their shells so shiny?

Snail varnish.

Ollie: When I grow up I want to be a pop star.
Mum: Make your mind up, you can't do both.

Which is faster, hot or cold?

Hot, because anyone can catch a cold.

How does the chicken-pox charity raise money?

With scratch cards.

A duck was waiting to cross the road when a chicken came running up and said, 'Don't do it, you'll never hear the end of it.'

Doctor: How old are you?

Patient: In a month I'll be seventy.

Doctor: Oh – I hope you haven't planned a party.

Customer: How much for a haircut?

Barber: Ten pounds

Customer: And how much for a shave?

Barber: Five pounds

Customer: Well, can you shave my head?

Wayne and Wesley are riding a tandem up a long hill. Eventually they reach the top.

Wesley says, 'That was very hard work.'

'Yes,' says Wayne, 'And steep – if I hadn't had the brakes on I think we'd have rolled all the way back down.'

What do you call a woman who keeps falling in the river?

Flo.

There's been an explosion at a pie factory.

Police say there were 3.14 casualties.

An eight-foot-tall man went for a job as a lifeguard.

'First things first, can you swim?' he was asked.

'No, but I can't half wade.'

Tarzan: I'm not feeling very well.

Doctor: Oh dear, say 'Aaaaaaaahhhhhhh!'

Diner: Waiter, my salad's completely frozen.

Waiter: That'll be the iceberg lettuce, sir.

Doctor: I want you to take the green pill with a glass of water at breakfast, the blue pill with two glasses of water at lunchtime and the red pill with a glass of water each night.

Patient: So what's my problem?

Doctor: You're not drinking enough water.

Wayne: Did you say I bring happiness wherever I go?

Amy: No, I said *when*ever you go.

Wayne: That horse you put a bet on has turned round and is running in the wrong direction.

Wesley: That's OK, I backed it both ways.

Who sits on a tractor shouting, 'The end is nigh!'?

Farmer Geddon.

What's nosy and ticks?

The neighbourhood watch.

'I tried to steal lasagne from the supermarket, but the female guard saw me. I couldn't get pasta.'

The online grocery store just texted to say they're out of pasta – which means we're penneless ...

Amy: Can I try on that dress in the window?

Assistant: If you like, but most people use the changing rooms.

Wayne: Why are you swimming backstroke all the time?

Wesley: I've just had my lunch and I don't want to swim on a full stomach.

F(x) walks into a bar and asks for a sandwich.

The landlord says, 'I'm sorry, we don't cater for functions.'

Bobby: Dad, I'm in the school orchestra playing the triangle.
Dad: Well, at least that'll give you some ting to do.

What do you call a magician's dog?
A Labracadabrador.

There are reports of big holes in the lawn in front of MI6's headquarters.

Everything points to them having a mole.

The trainee lumberjack was summoned to his boss's office. 'How come you're only cutting down ten trees a day?' he demanded.

'I don't know, boss, but I missed my training, I was ill.'

Hearing this, the boss calms down and takes him outside. 'OK, let's go through it again – give me your chainsaw.'

The trainee hands it over and the boss starts it up.

'Whoa,' says the trainee, 'what's that noise?!'

There were two flies on a bald man's head.

One says to the other: 'I remember when this was a footpath.'

What do you get if you divide the circumference of an apple by its radius?

Apple pi!

Knock, knock

Who's there?

Doctor

No, you can't get me with that one. You have to make online appointments now.

Where was the Magna Carta signed in 1215?

At the bottom.

Two prehistoric men were standing by Stonehenge. One says to the other: 'I can remember when all this was fields...'

First student: I copied my essay on the Black Death from the Internet.
Second student: Does that make you a bubonic plagiarist?

What happened to the lazy campers?

They were charged with loitering within tent.

Who cleans windows as he sings?

Shammy Davis Jr.

Which part of the ship do pirates like the least?
The poop deck.

What do apples and oranges have in common?

Neither of them are good at parallel parking.

A vicar paid a decorator to whitewash the church, but he thinned his paint down so much that the first time it rained, it all washed away. The vicar rang the decorator and complained.
'What do you want me to do about it?' asked the decorator.
'Repaint,' said the vicar, 'and thin no more.'

There's been an explosion at the factory which paints pillar boxes – a man is missing, presumed red.

Customer: I've had to come in to see you because you never answer the phone.

Assistant: What number have you been dialling, sir?

Customer: The one on your website – 0800 1800.

Assistant: They're our opening hours.

What do you get if you cross a vacuum cleaner with a door-to-door evangelist?

A Jehoover's Witness!

Wayne: My Granddad died at exactly 3:45 and at precisely the same time his grandfather clock stopped.

Wesley: That's amazing.

Wayne: Well, not really. That's when it fell on top of him.

Wayne: I read the other day that beer was bad for you, so I'm giving it up.

Wesley: What, you're giving up beer?

Wayne: No, I'm giving up reading.

———

Harry Potter's been having trouble with his wand, and since the repairer added lots of attachments it's got worse. It will now only cast a spell that makes people support a Lancashire football team. Bolt-on Wand-Errors.

Why did the chicken cross the Möbius strip?

To get to the same side.

Police have charged the World Scrabble champion for stealing high-scoring letters

She's expected to get a really tough sentence.

What do you call a fawn with a machine gun?
Bambo.

What do you give a forgetful cow?
Milk of amnesia.

What did one Dalek say to the other?

I've seen twelve different doctors now and none of them have had a clue what's wrong with me.

Four students went to a great party, overslept and missed an exam the next morning. They agreed to tell their professor they'd travelled in together and had a puncture on the way in that morning, which had caused them to be late, and asked if they could sit the exam the next day. The professor agreed.

The next morning they sat down and turned over the exam paper. It read: 'This exam consists of one question, worth 100 per cent. Which tyre had the puncture?'

How does Dick Dastardly find his way around?

With his Double Drat-nav.

Ollie: What has having kids taught you, Dad?

Dad: I suppose it's taught me patience, tolerance, self-denial, and lots of other things I wouldn't have needed if I hadn't had kids.

A woman approached a man in the pub thinking he'd been on *The Apprentice*, when in fact he'd appeared on *Big Brother*.

Police say it was a case of mistaken non-entity.

Wayne and Wendy were in their hotel room when the fire alarm went off. Wendy opened the door but the corridor was full of smoke.

'We'll have to jump out of the window,' said Wayne.

'But we're on the thirteenth floor,' pointed out Wendy.

'This is no time to be superstitious!'

Why did no-one want to work with the water pipe guy?

Because they found him deeply irrigating.

Two convicts were about to be executed and were asked if they had any last requests.

The first said he'd like to hear his favourite Justin Bieber song for the last time.

The second asked if he could be killed first.

A hiker was walking through the countryside when he saw a farmer holding a pig up to an apple tree while the pig ate the apples off it.

'Excuse me,' said the hiker, 'but wouldn't it be a lot quicker if you just shook the apples onto the floor.'

'Maybe,' said the farmer, 'but time's nothing to a pig.'

What's the best invention ever?

Window blinds – if it weren't for them it'd be curtains for everyone!

Paratrooper: What happens if my parachute doesn't open?

Sergeant: Bring it back and we'll give you a new one.

Which is a dog's favourite musical instrument?

The trombone

What do you call it when someone plays 'Waterloo' on a didgeridoo?

Abbariginal!

Customer: Hello, I'd like to book a room for next week.
Is it right you're a stone's throw from the beach?

Hotelier: Yes sir.

Customer: Lovely, and are you easy to find?

Hotelier: Yes, we're the one with the broken windows.

A large amount of hay has gone missing from some stables.
Police are making horse-to-horse enquiries.

How do you know when your house is almost full of toadstools?

There won't be mushroom inside.

Wesley: I think my wife's in for a letdown. She got all excited when I told her I was looking for cheap flights on the Internet.
Wayne: So?
Wesley: Well, she's never taken much interest in my darts up to now.

What did the sea monster say when it saw the submarine?

Oh no, tinned food again!

Big Ted: Do you want some pudding?

Little Ted: No, I'm stuffed.

What does the Army call a protective coat made entirely of oatmeal?

A flapjacket.

Wayne: It's puzzling me, every day when I get to my allotment, 'someone's spread a couple of inches of manure on it.

Wesley: Aha, the plot thickens.

'Doctor, I keep thinking I'm a lift.'

'Sounds like you're just coming down with something.'

Where in the Middle East do sheep fall out of the sky?

Baa-rain!

Dad: If you could choose to have a conversation with someone famous – either living or dead – who would you pick?

Son: The living one.

Did you hear that Oxygen and Magnesium have got together?

OMg!

If a fire hydrant has H_2O on the inside, what does it have on the outside?

K9P.

Have you heard about the band who were called 999 megabytes?

They still haven't got a gig.

Wayne: I haven't slept for five days.
Wesley: Well, neither have I ...
that would be far too long.

What happened when the billy goat and the nanny goat fell out?
They decided to stay together for the sake of the kids.

How do you make a pirate furious?

Take away the 'p'.

I used to live hand to mouth. Do you know what changed my life?

Cutlery.

Solicitor: Twenty pounds to cut my hair – but I'm nearly bald!
Barber: Yes, that includes a £15 search fee.

A lorry-load of nasal spray has overturned on the M25.

Police say there will be no congestion for twelve hours.

Where does a boxer keep the press cuttings of his best fights?
In a scrapbook.

What dresses in robes and runs through the desert with a bedpan and a lamp?
Florence of Arabia.

Amy: Have you noticed I bought a new toilet brush?
Frank: Yes, I tried it, but I think I prefer paper.

My wife said that I don't understand her and that I have no empathy.

I said, 'You've gotta be joking, no empty what...? And take that cough sweet out of your mouth...'

What are the the seven cars that cats love the best?

Fur-rari
Meowdi
Pawsche
Purrgeot
Mitsufishi
Mouse-cedes Benz
and a Squeaky Toyota

What happened to the idiot who tried to catch fog?

He mist

Girl: If you had two cars, would you give me one of them?
Boy: Yes.
Girl: And if you had two houses, would you give me one of them?
Boy: Of course I would.
Girl: What about if you had two chocolate bars?
Boy: That's not fair – you know I've got two chocolate bars!

We're renovating the house, and the ground floor is going really well. But the first floor? That's a different story.

What do you call an Australian prophet who absorbs the Ten Commandments?
Oz-Moses.

Wesley: I thought I'd take up ice fishing this winter?

Wayne: How did you get on?

Wesley: Terrible! I think the Zamboni machine kept scaring them away.

Wayne: I know you've been to the dentist, but what are those high notes coming from inside your mouth?

Wesley: That's my falsetto teeth.

How many men does it take to change a toilet roll?

Nobody knows, it's never happened.

First man: I've just started dating a twin.

Second man: Do you have any trouble telling them apart?

First man: Well, it helps that her brother has a beard.

———

Jane: Why do you call your cat Ben Hur?

Jill: Well, we used to call it Ben,
but then it had kittens.

———

**What's the difference between a useless
golfer and a useless skydiver?**

The golfer goes WHACK! 'Oh no!' whereas
with the skydiver it's the other way round.

Why are bowling alleys so quiet?

Because you can hear
a pin drop.

What's big, grey and runs away from the prince's grand ball?

Cinderellaphant.

What do alligators like to wear on their feet in muddy swamps?

Crocs.

Patient: My wife thinks I'm mad because I like sausages.

Doctor: I'm sure you're not mad – I love sausages.

Patient: Really? You must come and see my collection!

Diner: I'll have the fish – wait, I tell you what, make it a steak and kidney pie.

Waiter: The chef's not a magician, sir.

Doctor: It seems you've got pantomime syndrome.

Patient: Oh no I haven't.

How many tax inspectors does it take to screw in a lightbulb?

One. And the lightbulb is well and truly screwed.

Did you hear about the tourist in Spain who visited the Alhambra Palace 20 times?

He said it was very Moorish.

What athlete is warmest in the winter?

A long jumper.

I saw a documentary on how ships are kept together.

It was riveting.

Why shouldn't you buy a chess set from a pawn shop?

You'll only have half the pieces.

Philosophy lecturer: Who can tell me where satisfaction comes from?

Student: A satisfactory?

Who is the coolest person in hospital?

The ultra-sound guy.

And who's the coolest when he's away?

The hip replacement guy.

What do you call shoes made out of banana skins?

Slippers.

What happened to the butcher who backed into his bacon slicer?

He got a little behind in his work.

Teacher: Why did Mary and Joseph find no room at the inn?

Pupil: Because it was Christmas.

Boy: Dad, I think I dreamed in colour last night.

Dad: No, son, it was just a pigment of your imagination.

My wife accused me of being childish.

But I told her I was going to pedal my car exactly where I wanted to.

Patient: Doctor, I think I'm allergic to rice.
Doctor: You must be basmatic.

I'm proud to be American and I'm fed up with Europeans saying that America is 'the stupidest country in the world'.

Because in my opinion Europe is the stupidest country in the world.

A man was at the cinema and sat next to him was a boy with a dog. At the end of the film the dog started clapping.

'That's amazing,' said the man to the boy.

'It certainly is,' replied the boy. 'He hated the book.'

Hiker: Is it free to cross the field?

Farmer: No, the bull charges.

Where do fish keep their money?
In the riverbank.

Why are boxing rings square?

Where does a sick ship go?
To the dock.

Knock, knock.

Who's there?

Alec

Alec who?

Alec big buzzers and I cannot lie.

My annoying neighbour was banging on my door at three o'clock this morning.
Luckily I was still up practising my drums.

Why did the Mexican push his sister off a cliff?
Tequila!

Two old ladies were in church listening to a long sermon.
One leaned over and whispered to the other,
'My bottom is going to sleep.'
'I know,' replied her friend, 'I've heard it snoring!'

Why are there 32 letters in the pirate alphabet?

You have to remember there are seven 'C's

What's the difference between a financial adviser and someone reading this book?

One is all graphs and loans...

Mum: Put your coat on, I'm going out.
Dad You don't normally take me with you.
Mum: I'm not – I've just turned the heating off.

What has 100 legs and no teeth?

The front row of a Cliff Richard concert.

What's an orchestra conductor's favourite game?
Haydn seek!

Patient: Nurse, can I have a bedpan please?
Nurse: Sorry, I'm the head nurse.

Man: Have you found my lost dog yet?
Policeman: No, sir, we're still following all leads.

A man in a large shopping mall walked up to an attractive young woman.
'Excuse me,' he said, 'I can't seem to find my wife.'
'I'm sorry,' said the woman, 'but I don't see how I can help you.'
'Just keep talking to me,' said the man, 'she'll turn up in seconds.'

How do you organize a space party?
Planet!

What are the most beautiful valleys?

The ones that are gorges!

Dad: I got sent an email from someone who says he can read maps backwards.

Son: Dad, it's spam.

A man was passing a block of flats and saw a sign saying, 'Please ring bell for caretaker.' He rang it.

After a couple of minutes an old chap opened the door and asked, 'What do you want?'

'Nothing,' said the man. 'I've just rung the bell for you.'

Have you heard about the new 'Divorced Barbie'?

It comes with all Ken's stuff.

———

Wayne got a job with a telephone company, knocking telegraph poles in.

At the end of the day he went to get paid.

The foreman said, 'I can only pay you ten pounds, all the other workers have done ten times as many poles as you.'

'Yes,' said Wayne, 'but you should see how much they've left sticking out of the ground!'

———

Q: What do vegetarian's love best about Paris?

A: The Falafel Tower

What's worse than when it's raining cats and dogs?

Hailing taxis.

What kind of noise does a cat make driving a Formula 1 car?

"MiiiiiiiiaaaaoooooooooW!"

How do mountains hear things?
With their mountain ears.

Why did the clock scratch?
It had ticks.

Harry Potter: Don't be so hard on yourself, you're not bad-looking.

Hermione: I didn't say that. I said I'm feeling a bit Muggle-ly.

Two atoms left a restaurant, when one turned and said, 'I've got to go back, I've left an electron behind.'
'Are you sure?'
'Yes, I'm positive.'

Which sailor works at the Large Hadron Collider?
Bosun Higgs.

Wayne: I'm really excited, I'm going on a trip with the British Army's special forces. They're flying me all the way to Sweden!

Wesley: Really? Have you got a booking confirmation?

Wayne: Yes. Here it is.

Wesley: Right... that stands for Scandinavian Air Services.

Butcher: Can I interest you in eight legs of venison for £100?

Customer: No, that's too dear.

Why don't you see penguins in Britain?

They're afraid of Wales.

Who is sticky and sings?

Gluey Armstrong.

Who has a parrot that says, 'Pieces of two!'

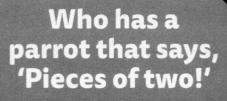

Short John Silver.

Doctor: We're going to put you in an isolation room and feed you pancakes and pizza.
Patient: Will that stuff cure me?
Doctor: No, but it's the only food we can slide under the door.

What holds the moon up in the sky?

Moonbeams!

Where do you get a dead heat with only one entry?

The crematorium.

What's a horse's favourite sort of food?

Oat cuisine.

Jack: I just used my donor card at the ATM instead of my bank card.

Jim: What happened?

Jack: It cost me an arm and a leg.

First man: I've just been to my friend's funeral – he was hit on the head by a tennis ball.

Second man: That's terrible news.

First man: Yes, but it was a beautiful service.

Why do people rarely go back to pancake houses in France?

They give them the crepes.

A woman went into a hairdressers in Newcastle and said, 'Can I have a perm, please?'

'Of course you can, pet,' said the Geordie, clearing her throat.

'I wandered lonely as a cloud...'

A farmer buys a talking sheepdog and decides to test him.

'Go into that field and count the sheep,' he says.

The dog comes back twenty minutes later.

'Forty sheep,' he says.

'You're not so clever,' says the farmer. 'There are only thirty-eight.'

'I know that,' said the sheepdog, 'I rounded them up.'

A man walked into a bookmaker's and asked,
'Is it true I can back a horse in here?'
'Of course you can.'
'Right lads! Back it in.'

Who's afraid of
Virginia Woolf?
Virginia Sheep!

What do convicts use
to talk to each other?
Cell phones!

Why do hipsters never burn their tongues?
Because they always wait till their food is coooool.

Teacher: Lucy, go to the map and find America.
Lucy: Here it is, miss.
Teacher: Good girl. Oliver, who discovered America?
Tommy: Lucy did, miss.

Which are the healthiest bees?

The Vitamin Bees.

What's purple, 5,000 miles long and full of pips?
The grape wall of China.

A man went to audition for a jazz band carrying two large bags full of various smartphones, Apple, Huawei, Samsung, Nokia, LG.

'You don't appear to have an instrument with you,' said the band leader.

'No, but I've got two sacks of phones.'

Son: Why is Mum cross with you, Dad?

Dad: No idea. She said she wanted something with diamonds for her birthday so I got her a pack of cards.

A man was zipping along a country lane in his sports car when, approaching a tight corner, a car came round the bend. As they passed closely, the lady driver of the other car wound down her window and shouted, 'Pig!'

The man, incensed, started to make all sorts of rude and offensive gestures in the direction of the disappearing car.

Then he hit the pig.

Son: Someone keeps pushing pieces of Plasticine through the letterbox.

Dad: Yes, I don't know what to make of it.

Boy: Dad, what's the difference between in-laws and outlaws?

Dad: Outlaws are wanted.

Why did Declan Donnelly hate being a pirate?

The captain kept shouting:
'All hands on deck!'

Oliver: My dad says he wants me to have all the educational opportunities he never had.

Jaden: So what's he doing?

Oliver: He's sending me to a girls' school.

What do you call a man with no shins?

Tony.

In which large body of water is it important to know EXACTLY where you are?

The Specific Ocean.

An overweight man went to see the doctor. The doctor said, 'I want you to eat regularly for two days, then skip a day, then eat regularly for two days, skip a day, then ring me in a fortnight.

A fortnight later the man rang the doctor. 'I've lost thirty pounds but it's nearly killed me.'

'Well, a lot of people find dieting hard,' said the doctor.

'It's not the dieting, it's all that skipping!'

I took my dog to the park today to play Frisbee with him.

But he was useless – I need a flatter dog.

What do you get when you cross a German composer with a bag of sugar?

A Schubert dip!

Why did the cat hijack a plane?

He wanted to go to the Canaries.

Knock, knock.

Who's there?

A wood wok

A wood wok who?

A wood wok 500 miles, and a wood wok 500 more!

A man and his wife went to a bar. After a few drinks he said 'I love you'.

'Is that you or the beer talking?' his wife asked.

'It's me talking to the beer...'

Patient: Doctor, I'm addicted to Twitter.

Doctor: I'm sorry, I don't follow you.

How can you tell a dyslexic Peaky Blinder?

He's got a cat-flap on his head.

A man goes to the doctor and says, 'You've got to listen to my leg, it keeps talking to me.'
The doctor puts his ear by the man's thigh, and hears: 'Lend me twenty pounds.'
He moves down to the knee: 'I'm skint, just let me have a tenner.'
Finally he reaches the shin: 'Please, a fiver, anything.'
The doctor stands up and says, 'I know what's wrong with you – your leg's broke in three places.'

Where did Noah keep his bees?

In the archives.

What do you call a man who lives with three cows, two goats, a pig and five chickens?
Barney.

First farmer: Why have you painted white lines between those four rows of cabbages?

Second farmer: It's a dual cabbage-way.

A ventriloquist at a club was making jokes about how stupid Premiership footballers are, when a man stood up.

'I'm a footballer and we're not all as stupid as you keep making out,' he shouted.

'I'm very sorry if I've offended you, sir,' said the ventriloquist.

'I'm not talking to you,' said the footballer, 'I'm talking to the little fella on your knee.'

What's the hardest train to catch?

The 12:50. Because it's only ten to one you'll catch it.

A breathless sailor dashes into the radio room to speak to the student radio operator. 'The ship's sinking! You've got to send an emergency message straight away!'

The student shrugs.

The man blurts out angrily: 'The one with the "O" in the middle!'

Student: 'All right. L.O.L.'

First man: I come from a long military family – my grandfather fell at Waterloo.

Second man: That's impossible, he wouldn't have been old enough.

First man: Someone pushed him off Platform 3.

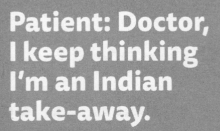

Patient: Doctor, I keep thinking I'm an Indian take-away.

Doctor: Well, Tarka dahl three times a day.

How many Oxford dons does it take to change a lightbulb?

Potesne quaerere illam quaestionem latine - quaesto non sonat satis momenti Aglice*

(*can you ask that question in Latin, it doesn't sound important enough in English.)

Teacher: Oliver, what is reincarnation?

Oliver: Is it where you die and come back as a tin of condensed milk?

Which cheese is made backwards?

Edam!

Son: Mum, is it true what Granny says, that Dad's a hard man to ignore?

Mum: Yes, son, but it's worth the effort.

It was really obvious that the solicitor had a will in his pocket.

It was a dead giveaway.

Q: Which is the worst French soccer manager to have as a next-door neighbour?

A: Arson Wenger.

Why did the ram run over the cliff?

He didn't see the ewe turn.

When you choke a Smurf, what colour does it turn?

It was a busy night in the Tarmac bar. Double yellow lines were drinking with disabled bays and Give Way markings. All of a sudden the bar went quiet as a piece of tarmac with a white bike painted on it walked in.

'What's up?' whispered a road cone to his friend.

'You don't want to mess with him,' came the reply.

'He's a cycle-path.'

What did the snail say when it rode on the tortoise's back?

Weeeeeeeeeeeeeeeeee!!!!!!!!!

What's the difference between a coyote and a flea?

One howls on the prairie and the other prowls on the hairy.

What happened when beavers re-wrote the script for the classic film 'Gone With the Wind'?

Scarlett O'Hara got less lines.

Where is Mozambique?

On the end of a Mozam-bird's face.

Teacher: Oliver give me a sentence starting with the word 'I'.

Oliver: I is –

Teacher: Stop right there. You should always, always, say, 'I am...'

Oliver: OK, then. I am the ninth letter of the alphabet.

What do you call a Dutchman who can brake from 100mph to a standstill in less than four seconds?

Max Verstoppen

First scientist: I've just managed to cross a homing pigeon with a Rottweiler.

Second scientist: I think that discovery will come back to bite you on the bum.

Teacher: Today we'll be looking at the alphabet and I'll be asking everyone what their favourite letter is.

Pupil: Please miss, my favourite letter is 'G'.

Teacher: And why is that, Angus...?

What do you call an aardvark that cries at sad films?

A vark.

———

Son: Do you want to come to those new shops with us?

Dad: No, once you've seen one shopping centre you've seen a mall.

Did you hear about the hippy at the rock festival who stayed up all night wondering where the sun had gone?

It finally dawned on him.

**Knock, knock.
Who's there?**
Figs
Figs who?
Figs the doorbell,
it's not working!

Lucy: I'm really fed up today – I think everyone hates me!
Mum: Don't be silly, dear. Everyone hasn't met you yet.

Boy: Mum, would you say Dad has a well-balanced personality?
Mum: Yes, he's got a chip on each shoulder.

Oliver: Why aren't you eating your animal biscuits?

Lucy: It said on the box, do not eat if the seal is broken.

What happens if you don't pay your exorcist?

You get repossessed.

A man went into a pub with a dog. 'I will bet anyone a hundred pounds that my dog can speak.'
Another man took the bet and the whole pub sat in silence for two minutes – including the dog.
The man left the pub humiliated and shouted at the dog, 'Why didn't you talk?'
'Relax,' said the dog, 'think of the odds we'll get tomorrow night.'

My window-cleaner's ladder has just got married.

He's pretty pleased because now he's got a step-ladder as well.

Where do gangsta grannies covered in jewellery go for a night out?

Blingo!

Q: What do you call a place that's halfway between murder and suicide...?

A: Merseyside

Bill and Bob were walking down the street when a mugger jumped out with a gun and demanded all their money.

As they emptied their pockets, Bill gave one note to Bob, saying: 'By the way, here's that tenner I owe you.'

Customer: Can you throw me the large salmon displayed in the window.
Fishmonger: Why do I have to throw it to you?

Customer: I've been fishing all day and I want to tell my friends I caught it.

How do pirates know what kind of weather is approaching?

They check their aye-aye-phones

Son: Why do you say marriage is like a pack of cards, Mum?

Mum: Well, at the start, all you need is a diamond and a pair of hearts ... after a few years you just want a club and a spade.

Mum: Go down the shop, son, get a bottle of milk, and if they've got eggs, get six.

Fifteen minutes later...

Mum: Why on earth have you bought six bottles of milk?

Son: They had eggs.

What does Doctor Who eat with his pizza?

Dalek bread.

Teacher: Name two crustaceans?

Pupil: Err, Kings Crustacean and Charing Crustacean.

An animal-loving Dad went up to a man in the park with a friendly-looking dog beside him.

'Does your dog bite?' asked Dad.

'No,' said the man.

Dad bent down to pat the dog, who suddenly snarled and gave him a nip on the hand.

'I thought you said your dog didn't bite?' asked Dad.

'That's not my dog,' replied the man.

What happened in the boxing match between the hedgehog and the mole?

The hedgehog won on points.

How does a rabbit get dry after its been raining?

He borrows a hare dryer.

Which is braver, a stone or a rock?

A rock, because it's a little boulder.

Boy in museum: How old is that stegosaurus skeleton?
Curator: It is 150 million years and six months old.
Boy: How can you be so accurate?
Curator: When I started here someone told me it was 150 million years old, and I've been here for six months.

Mum: You should go to see the doctor, you're addicted to drinking brake fluid.

Dad: No I'm not. And I can stop any time I want to.

First penguin: Ha, ha, you look like you're wearing a tuxedo.
Second penguin (enigmatically): Who says I'm not?

Knock, knock
Who's there?
A little old lady
A little old lady who?
I didn't know you could yodel!

Two old ladies were sitting in a café.
'The food here is terrible,' said the one.
'Yes, and such small portions,' agreed her friend.

Why was the calendar scared?

Because it knew its days were numbered.

What's the difference between a dad and a shopping trolley?

A shopping trolley has a mind of its own.

Two cows were in a field.

'Moo!' said one.

'That's exactly what I was going to say,' said the other.

Two owls were playing pool. The first owl was bending over a shot when his wing hit another ball.

'That's two hits,' said his friend.

'Two hits to who?' asked the first owl.

I'm having amnesia and Déjàvu at the same time.

I think I've forgotten this before.

A man went to the pub and ordered a pint of beer. As he sat drinking, he heard little voices saying, 'That's a nice jacket,' and 'Those glasses really suit you.'
The barman saw him looking puzzled and said, 'Don't worry, sir, the peanuts are complimentary.'

Why do divers fall out of the boat backwards to get into the water?

Because if they jumped forward they'd still be in the boat.

What should you do if your mouth ices up?

Grit your teeth.

What do you call it when a cat uses an apostrophe in the wrong place?

A catastrophe.

A white horse goes into a bar and asks for a beer.
'That's funny,' says the barman, 'we've got a
whisky named after you.'
'What,' says the horse, 'Roger?'

Why do squirrels swim on their backs?

To keep their nuts dry.

First farmer: Do your cows smoke?

Second farmer: No.

First farmer: In that case your barn is on fire.

Customer: Can I have a wasp, please?
Baker: Don't be daft, we don't sell wasps.
Customer: But you've got some in the window.

Who led the Pedant's Revolt?
Which Tyler.

Dad: Be honest, do you ever look at a man and wish you were single again?
Mum: Yes, every morning when I wake up.

Daughter: Mum, who's more clever – men or women?

Mum: Well, diamonds are a girl's best friend, and man's best friend is a dog – you work it out.

Teacher: Where was Hadrian's Wall built?
Pupil: Around Hadrian's garden.

Doctor: I don't know what you expect me to do for you, just because you're scared of Father Christmas.

Patient: I didn't say I was scared of Father Christmas, I said I'd got claustrophobia!

Patient: Doctor, I think I'm a kleptomaniac.

Doctor: Are you taking anything for it?

Patient: What's the prognosis, doc?

Doctor: Well, I wouldn't bother buying any green bananas if I were you.

Patient: Doctor, I think I've got athlete's voice.

Doctor: Don't you mean athlete's foot?

Patient: No, every time I sing, people run away.

There was uproar at the Badminton Horse Trials when one of the horses was found guilty ... of damaging wooden poles.

Luckily it was a first fence.

Son: Mum, does God use our bathroom?

Mum: No, why?

Son: Well, every morning Dad stands outside and says, 'God, how much longer are you going to be in there!?'

First kangaroo: I hope it doesn't rain today.

Second kangaroo: Why?

First kangaroo: The kids will want to play inside again.

A monastery falls on hard times so decides to open a fish and chip shop. At the grand opening, the first customer comes up to the man in a habit behind the counter and says, 'I suppose you're the fish friar!' 'No,' replies the man, 'I'm the chip monk!'

What's yellow and can't ski?

A bulldozer.

Boy: I'd like to buy a mouth organ please.
Shopkeeper: That's funny, I don't sell many but I had a girl in here only yesterday asking for the same thing.
Boy: That must have been our Monica.

What's a gazelle's favourite fruit?

An antelope melon.

There was very little interest in the origami club at work.

So it folded.

Charles Dickens went into a cocktail bar and ordered a Martini.

The barman said, 'Olive or twist?'

What did the scientist say when a lump of gold jumped onto his Periodic Table?

AU, get off my table!

What is the most common lie in the world?

'I have read and agree with the licence conditions.'

Who used to lurk in Sherwood Forest scaring pensioners?

Robin Hoodie.

What starts with 'e', ends with 'e' and only has one letter?

An envelope.

What's black and white and eats like a horse?

A zebra.

Colonel: Well, sergeant, there's bad news and good news. The bad news is, we're surrounded, outnumbered, low on ammunition, and only have horse manure to eat.
Sergeant: What's the good news?
Colonel: We've got absolutely loads of horse manure.

What's black and shiny and swashbuckling?

Binbag the Sailor.

Why do badgers dislike Wimbledon so much? They don't like going to five sets.

A little boy was sitting by the side of a drain in the road with a fishing rod. A little old lady went past and decided to humour him. 'How many have you caught?' she asked. **'You're the sixth,' he replied.**

Man: Someone's just stolen all my teacups.

Policeman: At least you haven't been mugged.

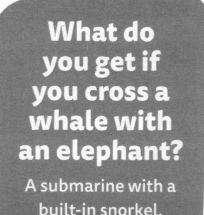

What do you get if you cross a whale with an elephant?

A submarine with a built-in snorkel.

What cheese do you use to entice Paddington out of his house?

Camembert.

Maths teacher: Why haven't you done your homework on decimals, Lucy?

Lucy: I couldn't see the point.

What did Obi Wan-Kenobi say to Luke Skywalker when he kept eating with his fingers?

Use the fork, Luke!

Dad: My personal trainer says that I should do lunges to keep in shape.
He says that would be a big step forward.

Why was the toothpaste late?

It got held up in the Tube!

A man looked over his fence and saw the neighbour's little boy digging a hole.

'What are you digging that hole for, sonny?'

'I'm burying my pet mouse.'

'That's a big hole for a mouse.'

'Well, it's inside your cat.'

Customer: I just played this vinyl record and all I could hear was a loud buzzing.

Record-shop assistant: Ah, you must have been playing the Bee-side.

Two ostriches fall out and the big one starts chasing the small one. Just as he's about to catch him, the little ostrich sticks his head in the sand. 'That's strange,' says the big ostrich, coming to a halt. 'Where did he go?'

What do bees sing in a recession?

'Honey's Too Tight To Mention.'

Stewardess: Would you like dinner, sir?
Passenger: What are my choices?
Stewardess: Yes or no.

I knew it was raining cats and dogs so I took an umbrella. Then I stepped in a poodle...

French knock-knock joke:
Frappe, frappe.
Qui est la?
L'ost.
L'ost qui?
Oui.

A man went into a chemist's and asked if they had anything for hiccups. The assistant immediately slapped him round the face.
'What did you do that for?' asked the man.
'You're not hiccupping now, are you?' said the assistant.
'No, but my wife is and she's outside in the car.'

A woman was in a library when she saw a man playing chess with a dog. 'That's one clever dog,' she said to the man. 'Not really,' said the man. 'He gets all his moves from a book.'

What do you give dead bread?

A toast mortem.

What's green and can't ski?

A John Deere bulldozer.

Doctor: How's that patient coming along who swallowed all those coins?

Nurse: No change yet, I'm afraid.

Patient: How much to remove my tooth?

Dentist: £200.

Patient: And how long will it take?

Dentist: About ten minutes.

Patient: £200 for ten minutes!

Dentist: I can make it last an hour if you'd prefer.

What do you call an owl wearing a toupee?

Hedwig.

First man: I slept like a log last night.

Second man: That's good.

First man: Not really, I woke up in the fireplace.

Winnie the Pooh is popular around the world, but the word 'Pooh' doesn't translate very well into foreign languages. So in France he is known as *Winnie l'Ours*, (Winnie the Bear). In Italy he is Winnie l'Ourso, in Spain, Winnie el Oso, in Germany, Winnie der Bär, and in China, Xi Jing Ping.

Mum: Where shall we go on holiday next year?
Dad: I'd like to go somewhere I've never been before.
Mum: How about the kitchen?

What do they call an upside-down cake in Australia?
A cake.

Patient: I keep seeing spots before my eyes.

Doctor: Have you seen an optician?

Patient: No, just spots.

Two mathematicians had been struggling to work out the height of a long pole leaning against a wall.
Eventually an engineer came by and offered to help. He took hold of the pole, lay it on the ground and measured it with a tape.
'Typical engineer,' said the mathematicians.
'We wanted the height and he gave us the length.'

Julius Caesar loved chocolate biscuits and put six on a plate for when his friend Brutus came to tea. Caesar nipped off to the toilet and when he came back there were only four left on the plate, so he accused him 'Ate two, Bruté...?

God and Satan are in dispute about the boundary between heaven and hell. Eventually God threatens to take Satan to court.
'Oh yes,' said Satan, 'and where are you going to find a lawyer?'

Why couldn't the owl go out with his girlfriend in the rain?

Because it was too wet to woo.

A journalist was being shown around the most hi-tech computer centre in the world by its owner.

'It's so advanced we only employ one man and one dog,' said the owner.

'What's the man's job?' asked the reporter.

'To feed the dog.'

'So what's the dog's job?'

'He's there to stop the man touching the computer.'

Why were Tinkerbell's wings so tired?

Because all the signs around her said 'Never Land'.

As an experiment I took both sides off my ladder.

I didn't like it. Now it just looks all rung.

First scientist: My desk keeps disappearing and coming back.

Second scientist: Ah, you must have a periodic table.

What kind of sentence would you get for breaking the law of gravity?

A suspended one.

Dad: I saw my old girlfriend last night – apparently she hasn't stopped drinking since I broke up with her ten years ago.

Mum: You'd have thought she'd have stopped celebrating by now.

What are a dentist's favourite two letters?

DK.

Why do people distrust throat lozengers so much?

Because some of them
are totally menthol!

Receptionist: Doctor, there's a man here who says he thinks he's invisible.

Doctor: Tell him I can't see him.

First man: My dog's always chasing people on bicycles.

Second man: Well, lock his bicycle up then.

A man was at the Superbowl and was surprised to see an empty seat beside him. He asked the man on the other side of the seat if he knew whose it was.

'Well,' said the man, 'my wife and I have always wanted to come to the Superbowl, and this year we finally managed to get tickets. But unfortunately, recently she was run over by a bus and died.'

'That's awful,' said the first man. 'But isn't there a friend or relation who could have come with you?'

'No, they're all at the funeral.'

Did you hear about the man who bought a pair of tortoiseshell shoes?

It took him two hours to get out of the shop.

Mum: What were you doing last night in bed? You kept shouting about hobbits and elves.

Dad: Sorry, I must have been Tolkien in my sleep.

What is the sporting highlight of an owl's year?

The Superb-owl

Why are hotel bibles like squirrels?

There are millions of them but very few are red.

Two brothers went to enlist in the armed forces.
'Have you got any special skills?' the first one was asked.
'I'm a pilot,' he replied, and was immediately signed up.
Then they asked the other brother the same question.
'I chop wood,' he said. He was rejected.
'But you took my brother on,' he protested.
'Yes, but he's a pilot.'
'Well, he can't pile it until I've chopped it, can he?'

First man: I've just seen an amazing bloke.
He emptied a toolbox and chopped the
tools into little pieces using his teeth.
Second man: That's incredible. Was he a
professional strongman?
First man: No, he's a hammer-chewer.

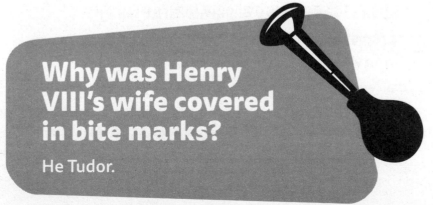

Why was Henry VIII's wife covered in bite marks?

He Tudor.

Why is bullfighting a safe profession? There's only one danger, and that's avoid-a-bull.

What do you get if you cross a yeti and a vampire? Frostbite.

A man was caught stealing milk, vanilla essence and cornflour from the supermarket

He was remanded in custardy.

The vicar was strolling round his parish when he came upon old Joe tending his lovely garden. 'Isn't it wonderful, Joe,' he said, 'to see what beauty man and the Lord can achieve when they work together.' **'I suppose so,' said Joe, 'but you should have seen the state of it a few years ago when God was looking after it on his own.'**

Patient: Doctor, I think I've got Dutch flu.

Doctor: What do you mean?

Patient: Well, I'm all clogged up.

Why do demons and ghouls stick together?

Because demons are a ghoul's best friend.

How do we know Robinson Crusoe was efficient?

He had all his work done by Friday!

Diner: Waiter, there are no strawberries in my strawberry cheesecake.

Waiter: Well, there's no angels in the angel cake either, and don't get me started on the Black Forest Gateau!

What happened after the two jars of Marmite got married?

They had twiglets.

Q: What happened to the man who fell into an upholstery machine?

A: He's fully recovered.

Son: Do you want the good news or the bad news?

Dad: What's the good news?

Son: The airbags work on the car.

When are you going to put those shelves up?

Dad: Stop nagging, I said I'll do it and I will.

You don't have to keep reminding me every six months.

What goes 'Buzz, zzub, buzz, zzub ...'?

A bee glued to a yo-yo.

First continental plate: There's just been a big earthquake.

Second continental plate: Well it wasn't my fault!

A man staggered home the worse for wear with a duck under his arm.

'Don't you bring that pig in here,' said his wife.

'In case you hadn't noticed,' said her husband, 'it's a duck.'

'I was talking to the duck.'.

How do you de-ice a cloud?

Use a skyscraper.

Man: Every time the doorbell rings our dog runs into a corner.

Vet: Well, of course he does, he's a boxer.

Theatre director: I've just auditioned your wife for *Oedipus the King*.
Friend: Jocasta?
Director: No, she was terrible.

What do you call a man with a pole through his leg?

Rodney.

Sherlock Holmes and Dr Watson returned home one night to find themselves locked out of their flat. Watson went off to find Mrs Hudson but when he returned Holmes had already let himself in with a key he'd fashioned from a piece of fruit.

'How on earth did you do it, Holmes?' he asked.

'Lemon entry, my dear Watson.'

What do you call a rabbit with fleas?

Bugs Bunny.

What's the last thing that goes through a fly's mind when it hits a car windscreen?

Its anus.

How much do seagulls get paid?

Nothing, they have to survive on tips.

What did the book reviewer say about the world's heaviest book?
'I couldn't pick it up.'

What do you call a fawn who keeps surprising people?
Bamboo.

Teacher: Did you read that book about glue, Lucy?
Lucy: I couldn't put it down.

An idiot is walking along a river bank, wondering how to get across. On the opposite bank he sees another idiot.
'Hey,' he shouts, 'how can I get to the other side?'
'You're already on the other side!'

Why was the plastic bag put in quarantine for six months?
They thought he might be a carrier.

Who is a pirate's all-time favourite *Star Wars* character?

Arrrrrrrrr- 2-D-2*

*not the Mandal-Oar-ian

Wesley: I'm reading this best-selling anti-gravity book?

Wayne: Is it any good?

Wesley: I just can't put it down!

What does the 'Dentist of the Year' receive?

A little plaque.

A soccer referee wants to learn a musical instrument. He walks into a music shop and after much deliberation he says, 'I'll have the red trumpet and the white accordion please.'

The shop owner says, 'I can sell you the fire extinguisher if you like, but the radiator *has* to stay.

An Englishman, a Frenchman, a Turk, an Iraqi, an Indian, a Korean, an Australian, and a Mexican decided to visit a posh restaurant.

The doorman stopped them on the way in and said, 'I'm sorry, gentlemen, but you can't come in here without a Thai.'

What's the best way to serve turkey?

Join the Turkish Army.

What did Big Ben say to the Leaning Tower of Pisa?

I've got the time if you've got the inclination!

Customer: Have you any invisible ink?

Assistant: Certainly sir, what colour?

How does Long John Silver keep fit?

Aye, Gym, lad!

Lucy: My budgie died of flu yesterday, miss.
Teacher: Was it bird flu?
Lucy: No, he flew into the lawnmower.

Why is it so difficult to teach dogs to dance?

They've got two left feet.

Why can't pigs talk to one another on the phone?

There's too much crackling.

In the woods, a baby squirrel kept throwing himself off a tree branch, flapping his legs furiously. Every time he crashed to the ground, and every time he would climb back up and jump off again.

Two birds were watching the scene, and eventually one turned to the other and said, 'I think it's time we told him he was adopted.'

How do you get a student out of the shower?
Turn it on.

How do you get a student into the shower?
Put a beer in it.

Where does Kylie get her kebabs from?

Jason's Doner Van.

Patient: Doctor, I've just swallowed a camera.

Doctor: Well, come back next week and we'll see what develops.

Wayne and Wesley are walking along a road when they see two other men coming towards them with a bag full of fish. 'How did you catch them?' asked Wayne.

'My friend dangled me over the bridge by my legs and I caught the fish as they swam up river.'

They decide to give it a try. They got to the bridge and Wayne lowered Wesley down. He'd been dangling there for five minutes when he shouted, 'Quick, pull me up, pull me up!'

'Have you caught a fish?'

'No, there's a train coming!'

What did Arnold Schwarzenegger say when his wife asked him if Christmas was his favourite holiday?

I still love Easter, baby!

If a cross between a Labrador dog and a Poodle is a 'Labradoodle'. What do you call a cross between a Great Dane and a Chihuahua?
Unlikely.

A square and a circle go into a pub.
The square said, 'Your round.'

What do you call a Premiership footballer in a suit?

The defendant.

Policeman: Do you know why I've pulled you over, sir?

Motorist: It depends... How long have you been following me?

Oliver was helping his Dad with some D-I-Y.

'You're like lightning with that hammer, Ollie,' said his dad.

'I am pretty quick' said Oliver

'No, it's just you never strike twice in the same place.'

Interviewer: I'll give you the job if you can answer this question: which bird doesn't build its own nest?

Wayne: The cuckoo.

Interviewer: Well done, you'd be surprised how many people don't know that.

Wayne: Yeah – people forget they live in clocks.

Terrorists hijacked a plane full of international bankers.

They issued a statement saying that they would release one banker every hour until their demands were met.

How does a lawyer get to sleep?
First he lies on one side, then he lies on the other.

How do we know Moses was a Dad?

He was lost in the wilderness for forty years and never asked for directions once.

Wayne: Can I buy a green Stars and Stripes please?
Shopkeeper: I'm sorry, they only come in red, white and blue.
Wayne: All right, I'll have a blue one.

What happened when the depressed man bought himself a scooter?

He moped around all day.

Musician: Did you hear my last performance?

Music Critic: I hope so.

The god of thunder was out for a ride on his favourite horse, the wind rushing through his hair.

'I Am Thor!' he shouted up to the sky.

'Well,' said his horse, 'next time bring your thaddle, thilly!'

What do you get if you cross a parrot, an umbrella and a goat?

Polyunsaturated butter!

What is the longest piece of furniture in a school?

The multiplication table.

**What did one mayfly
say to another mayfly?**
Have a nice day!

**How do you mend
a cracked parrot?**
With polly-filler.

What do you call a gunfighter who drinks nothing but lemonade?

Wyatt Burp.

**A man went to see a lawyer and asked him
what his fee was.**
'I charge £500 for three questions,' said the lawyer.
'Isn't that a bit greedy?' asked the man.
'Yes it is, what's your final question?'

Why did the useless golfer's wife have him buried beneath his own father?

She said finally he'd be under Pa!

Son: Do you know where the yeast extract is, Pa?

Dad: No, but Ma might.

What's the difference between Dad's old car and a golf ball?

You can drive a golf ball 250 yards.

Did you hear about the man who lived in a car tyre?
He had a puncture and now he lives in a flat.

First tramp: I see you've lost a shoe.
Second tramp: No, I've found one.

What should you do with dead radiographers?

Barium.

Sacha: Why did you break it off with that tennis player?

Kelly: I had to – love meant nothing to him.

Man: Tell me, darling, do you like rings?
Woman: Oh, yes!
Man: Good, I've entered you for the boxing tournament on Saturday.

I'm really good friends with almost all the letters of the alphabet.

I just don't know Y.

What's a beaver's all-time favourite musical?

Riverdance.

What do you get if you cross an ape with a set of drums?

A timpanzee.

How does old MacDonald communicate?

By e-i-e-i-o-mail.

First man at funeral: Twenty clowns at that circus, and poor Buttons was the most popular – I can't believe they've only sent one car of mourners.

Second man: Ah, but just wait and see how many get out of it.

Why is a lamppost heavy at the bottom?

Because it's light at the top.

**Boy: Mum, Dad says he's in shape,
is that true?**

Mum: Well ... I suppose round is a shape.

**Son: Mum, do we get vegetable oil from
vegetables and sunflower oil from sunflowers?**

Mum: Yes, son, that's right.

Son: So where do we get baby oil from?

A horse goes into a bar and says, 'Can I have a large aperitif, please.' The barman says, 'They look large enough to me already.'

Teacher: Can you all hear the fire alarm?

Pupil: Is it a drill, sir?

Teacher: No, you idiot, it's a bell.

Son: Dad, I don't like this Swiss cheese, it's got holes in it

Dad: Well, eat the cheese and leave the holes on the side of your plate.

Divorce judge: Mr Smith, I have decided to award your wife £200 per week.

Smith: That's very good of you, your honour. I'll try and slip her a few quid myself when I'm flush..

How did Moses see in the desert at night?

He turned on the Israelites.

Oliver: Do you know why the Army have called their new gun 'the teacher'.

Teacher: No, why?

Oliver: Because it doesn't work and can't be fired

Why are Russian dolls arrogant?

Because they're always full of themselves.

Doctor: Now, how's your broken rib coming along?

Patient: Well, I've started getting a stitch in my side.

Doctor: Good, that means the bone is knitting.

Two men sitting next to each other on a plane strike up a conversation and start swapping jokes.

'I've got a brilliant teacher joke,' says one.

'I'd better let you know,' said the other, 'I'm a teacher myself.'

'Don't worry,' said the joker, 'I'll tell it really slo-o-w-wly.'

Where do beavers buy all their chunky boots?
Timberland.

Why are beavers like large national banks?
They're always removing branches.

Patient: Doctor, I keep thinking I'm a bridge.

Doctor: What's come over you?

Patient: Seven cars, two buses and a truck...

What's the nose-blowing capital of the UK?

It's Nottingham!

Why was the uninhibited librarian sacked?

She had no shelf-control.